SPEND A D OLD POMPEII

A Kid's Guide To Ancient Pompeii, Italy

PHOTOGRAPHY BY JOHN D. WEIGAND
POETRY BY PENELOPE DYAN

Bellissima Publishing, LLC
Jamul, California
www.bellissimapublishing.com

ISBN 978-1-935630-01-2
First Edition

For Kids Who Love To Learn
And For Parents Who Love
To Learn With Them!

Spend A Day In Old Pompeii

Bellissima Publishing, LLC

Introduction

The Roman city of Pompeii was destroyed by a volcanic eruption in 79 A.D.   It was first occupied in 6th century B.C, and the Romans turned it into a place to vacation in 81 B.C., and it served that purpose (among others) until it was buried, lost, and forgotten under mud and ash.

Two million people now live under Mount Vesuvius, and it has erupted more than fifty times since 9 A.D.. It continued to erupt every 100 years until about 1037 A.D., when it went into hibernation for six hundred years. In 1631, Mount Vesuvius erupted yet again, taking 4000 more lives. During the restoration (after the 1631 eruption) workers discovered the ruins of ancient Pompeii!

Everyone is curious about Pompeii, because the city was a wonderful, glamorous and modern place that seemed to just disappear (like the tale of Atlantis) from the face of the earth. This is your chance to see a bit of exactly what has been uncovered, as John D. Weigand's photographs and the poetry of Penelope Dyan help you explore this once great and ancient city in the pages of yet another Bellissima book meant for kids that looks great on your coffee table!

Spend A Day In Old Pompei

Bellissima Publishing, LLC

Spend A Day In Old Pompeii

A Kid's Guide To Ancient Pompeii, Italy

PHOTOGRAPHY BY JOHN D. WEIGAND
POETRY BY PENELOPE DYAN

Once upon a time far, far away
There was a place they called Pompeii.
And behind the city you could see if you looked around,
Mount Vesuvius stood silently not making a sound.

They had water jugs and marked their graves with stone,
And people came to vacation from faraway Rome.

They had roads and used stepping stones to cross the street, and when the roads flooded with water, they had dry feet.

And every time you looked around,
Down the road was Mount Vesuvius not making a sound.

It hovered over Pompeii city fair,
And it could be seen from everywhere.

Beyond the pillars and the city wall,
Mount Vesuvius stood strong and tall.
Until one day in 79 A.D. it rumbled and grumbled
and from inside it ash and fire blew and tumbled.

And the truth is you can never really know when
Mount Vesuvius will raise her voice and be heard again.
And the ground will shake and she will rumble and grumble.
From the top of that mountain the fire ash will AGAIN tumble.

You can see where the chariots left their tracks at Pompeii,
While Mount Vesuvius stood rumbling from not far away,

And you can see the public bath
(where MEN bathed TOGETHER)
Now PLEASE DO NOT laugh.

And when they were finished with bathing for the day,
They went out for fast food in ancient pompeii,
Because no one had a kitchen at home,
And I suppose they NEVER EVER ate all alone.

You can see the bakery where the donkeys ground wheat,
going round and round to make flour for the oven,
that cooked bread dough tasty sweet.

And if you wee very lucky you could take your bread home,
and then step right into a sunken bath of your own.

The Temple of Iris stands in Pompeii,
uncovered and unearthed so we can see it today!
And you can see other temples in Pompeii and statues and stuff,
And of this place you can NEVER get enough.

And here is the most interesting thing of all. . .
a grant mural uncovered and PAINTED on a wall!

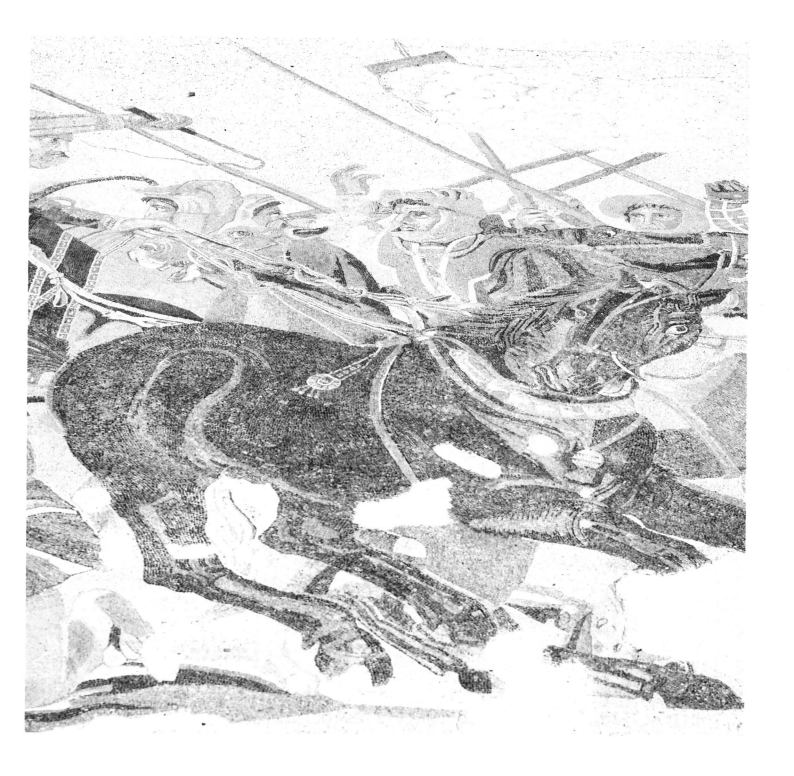

You might say everyone lived in happiness and bliss,
until Mount Vesuvius exploded and left them like this,

Everything stopped and was frozen in time and space. And Pompeii was under the power of Mount Vesuvius. And Pompeii was a frightening, terrible place.

And now archeologists have dug up the past.
And it seems that some things were just meant to last.

And you can see those people were like us and the same,
And for what happened to them we have only nature to blame.
It was the work of the mountain behind them so tall,
that finally and forever sealed the fate of them all.

And now among the rubble of this once lavish place,
we can learn from these people who for us have no face.

And as they and their things are removed
from the dust of the land,
behind them stands Mount Vesuvius
still standing high and so grand,

And as the hunt is on, and archeologists restore this place,
it all serves as a tribute to the great human race. . .
It's a tribute to how we can rise from the ashes and fly,
as Pompeii is explored under the warm sunny sky.